2 ox 9|09

THE CIVIL WAR
1840s ~ 1890s

BY
ROGER E. HERNÁNDEZ

Marshall Cavendish
Benchmark
New York

Thanks to Stephen Pitti, professor of history and American studies at Yale University, for his expert reading of this manuscript.

MARSHALL CAVENDISH BENCHMARK
99 WHITE PLAINS ROAD
TARRYTOWN, NEW YORK 10591-5502
www.marshallcavendish.us

Text copyright © 2009 by Marshall Cavendish Corporation

All Web sites were available and accurate when this book was sent to press.

LIBRARY OF CONGRESS CATALOGING-IN-PUBLICATION DATA
Hernández, Roger E.
The Civil War, 1840s-1890s / by Roger E. Hernández.
p. cm. — (Hispanic America)
Includes bibliographical references and index.
ISBN 978-0-7614-2939-5
1. Hispanic Americans—History— 19th century—Juvenile literature.
2. Hispanic Americans—Biography—Juvenile literature.
3. United States—Ethnic relations—History—19th century—Juvenile literature.
4. United States—History—Civil War, 1861-1865—Participation, Hispanic American—Juvenile literature.
I. Title.
E184.S75H475 2008
973.70868—dc22
2007049525

Photo research by Linda Sykes

Cover photo: The Battle of Glorieta Pass" by Roy Andersen, artist. Courtesy Pecos National Historical Park, National Park Service
The photographs in this book are used by permission and through the courtesy of:
Texas State Library and Archives: 1, 31; Anaheim Public Library: 4; Webb Heritage.org: 10; Corbis: Bettmann, 13, 56; ©Corbis, 15; ©Christie's Images, 33; ©Wolfgang Kaehler, 60; Jean-Pierre Arnet, Sygma, 53; Underwood & Underwood, 69. Alamy: North Wind Pictures, 16, 48; AA World Travel Library, 64. Library of Congress: 18. Museum of New Mexico, Palace of the Governors: 22, 23. The Granger Collection: 26, 38, 41, 44, 51, 65, 71, back cover. Collection of the Witte Museum, San Antonio, Texas: 28, 34. California Ethnic and Multicultural Archives, Dept. of Special Collections, Donald Davidson Library, University of California, Santa Barbara, CA: 45. Bancroft Library, University of California, Berkeley, CA: 46. Courtesy Key West Art and Historical Society: 62. The Florida Memory Project Florida State Library and Archives: 67.

EDITOR: Joy Bean   PUBLISHER: Michelle Bisson
ART DIRECTOR: Anahid Hamparian   SERIES DESIGNER: Kristen Branch

Printed in China
1 3 5 6 4 2

Contents

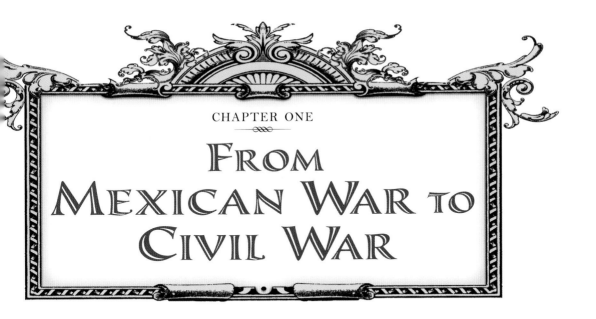

CHAPTER ONE

FROM MEXICAN WAR TO CIVIL WAR

M OST *HISPANIC* FAMILIES HAVE LIVED IN THE United States for only a few decades, but not all are such recent immigrants. Some Hispanics were already living in the United States early in the nineteenth century, even before the height of immigration from Europe. A number of new Hispanic immigrants settled in New York, and later in Florida, to escape from the Spanish colonial regime that ruled Cuba and Puerto Rico at that time. The majority, however, lived in the Southwest.

After the U.S.-Mexican War (1846-1848) ended with the Treaty of Guadalupe Hidalgo, the United States took unchallenged possession of what are now the modern-day states of

Opposite:
Some Hispanics have been living in the United States since the nineteenth century.

Arizona, California, Colorado, Nevada, New Mexico, Texas, and Utah. Today, all those states, except for California, make up the American Southwest, and are home to more than 75 million people. In 1848, that region was sparsely populated. Some inhabitants were Native Americans, from tribes including the Pueblo, Apache, and Navajo. Others were *Anglos*—the non-Hispanic Caucasian Americans whose armies had won the war and forced Mexico to *cede* them the territories they controlled. Still others were Hispanics who had lived in the area when it belonged to Mexico and, before that, Spain. Those Hispanics found that the signing of the treaty meant their homes were now on American soil.

After the war ended, the Mexican Hispanics wanted to be treated as American citizens, with the same rights that Anglos enjoyed. Unfortunately, some Anglos looked down on Hispanics. The war had been launched by the United States with a sense of *Manifest Destiny*, the notion that the United States was destined to expand westward to the Pacific Ocean. In parts of the Southwest, former citizens of Mexico were reduced to taking low-paying jobs, excluded from political power, displaced from their lands, considered bandits, or even lynched.

For example, by the year 1856, the city of San Antonio, Texas, "had been half-deserted by its *Mexicano* population," historian David Montejano wrote in his book *Anglos and Mexicans in the Making of Texas*. Texas Anglos saw the largely mixed-race Mexicans as different from themselves. Stephen F. Austin, who founded the first Anglo-American colony in Texas, in 1822 while it still belonged to Mexico, said that the Texas War of Independence, in which he was a leader, pitted "a mongrel Spanish-Indian and negro race, against civilization and the Anglo-American race, as historian Arnoldo De León wrote in *The Tejano Community, 1836-1900*. Mexicans often were shut out of skilled jobs, such as tailors and stonemasons. Many became laborers or servants instead. Mexicans were also forced out of their jobs transporting goods between inland Texas and the Gulf Coast. In the Cart War of 1857, some seventy-five Mexican carters were killed on orders of Anglos who then took over their business.

Mariano Vallejo and his family were instrumental in developing California as a state in the Union.

The new Americans did not always fare so badly, however. In California, Hispanic political leaders like Pablo de la Guerra, a landowner and judge, and General Mariano Vallejo, who had been a military commander under Mexican rule, helped write the state constitution in 1849, and they won the right for the state to continue publishing laws in both Spanish and English. However, they failed to preserve the Mexican and Spanish legal tradition that taxes should be collected at the local rather than statewide level.

During the nineteenth century, Hispanics succeeded best in New Mexico, which had the largest and oldest Spanish-speaking population, already established when New Mexico became a U.S. territory in 1850. The elite of this group, direct descendants of the Spanish colonists of the seventeenth and eighteenth centuries, were traditionally called *Hispanos*. They continued to be prominent in politics, culture, and to a lesser extent, the business world outside of ranching. Yet Hispanos fell behind in one important way: it took more than half a century for New Mexico to become a state.

THE SOUTHWEST IN THE CIVIL WAR

One reason for the delay in statehood for New Mexico was that New Mexico's Anglo and Hispanic politicians rejected a plan backed by Miguel A. Otero, a New Mexican delegate in Congress. The plan offered statehood in exchange for entering the Union (the United States) as a slave state. In the years leading to the U.S. Civil War (1861-1865), that was one of several arguments dividing the Northern and Southern states: the issue of allowing slavery in territories newly admitted to the Union.

Once the war started, New Mexico's territorial governor, Henry Connelly, tried to rally Hispanics to the Union cause by portraying Confederates (the seceding Southerners called themselves the Confederate States of America) as the enemy, or the equivalent of those Anglos in Texas who held Hispanics in contempt.

Some Hispanics in the Southwest were indifferent about taking sides in the Civil War. They had been part of the United States for just thirteen years—not enough time to see themselves as part of their new nation.

In New York, the situation was a little different. One group of Cubans living there had already been allied with Southerners as far back as the 1850s, over a decade before the Civil War, because of the politics of their homeland. They wanted Cuba to be independent from Spain without having to free slaves, and thought that the best way to achieve both goals was for Cuba to become a slave state. Their contacts in the American South also wanted Cuba to join the Union as a slave state, because it would give the South more force in Congress.

"U.S. Latino Patriots," a study by Pew Hispanic Center, a research organization in Washington, D.C., reported that at the start of the Civil War, some 2,550 Mexican Americans joined Confederate military units and another 1,000 joined Union forces. By the end of the conflict, said the Pew study, some 9,000 Hispanic troops had fought on one side or the other of the Civil War. A number of Hispanics became officers, and most rank-and-file soldiers served alongside Anglos in integrated regiments, although some units were made up largely of Hispanic soldiers.

Among those in mostly Hispanic units was Santos Benavides, who commanded the Confederacy's 33rd Texas Cavalry. He is remembered for leading the successful defense of his home city of Laredo—which his great-great grandfather had founded—with forty-two troops against an attacking force of two hundred Union soldiers. His victory allowed the South to keep open vital routes used to trade cotton with Mexico. Benavides, who reached the status of colonel, was the highest-ranking Mexican American in Confederate uniform.

Another largely Hispanic military unit in the cavalry was created by the Union to take advantage of the extraordinary horsemanship of *Californio vaqueros*, or Hispanic cowboys from California. This cavalry battalion, commanded by Major Salvador Vallejo, brother of the Californio politician who helped write the state constitution, "guarded supply trains, chased bandits, fought Confederate raiders," according to the Pew report. In at least one case, *bandidos* and Confederate raiders were one and the same—the *vaquero* cavalry tried but ultimately failed to apprehend John Mason and Jim Henry, who robbed stage coaches in southern California while claiming to be Confederate guerrillas. Later, the unit served as far away as Arizona, helping to defeat a Confederate invasion of New Mexico.

Colonel Santos Benavides was the highest-ranking Tejano soldier to serve in the Confederate military.

The Confederate invasion of New Mexico started in 1861, when a force of Texan troops marched into the neighboring state and conquered the city of Albuquerque and the capital of Santa Fe. For several months, the Confederate flag flew over the seventeenth-century Spanish Palace of the Governors. But New Mexico roused enough Union troops, including Hispanics, to fight back. The Second Regiment of New Mexico, as well as six other *militia* companies, were formed in the state. Most of the approximately four thousand troops and officers were Mexican Americans, as were some of their commanders, such as Lieutenant Colonel Manuel Chávez and General Stanilus Montoya.

These local militias took part in crucial engagements in March of 1862. With New Mexico's capital occupied by the Confederacy, Union troops and local militia fought the Confederates at Apache Canyon, east of Santa Fe. The Confederate force of more than two hundred Texans withdrew to defensive positions at nearby Glorieta Pass in the Sangre de Cristo, or Blood of Christ, Mountains, an area of Hispanic settlement in New Mexico since Spanish colonial times. Both sides received reinforcements, bringing the number of troops to about one thousand each. Then a Union force led by Colonel Chávez slipped behind enemy lines by sliding down on ropes from the top of a cliff, and set fire to the Confederate's supply wagons. Without supplies, the rebels could not hope to hold on, so they retreated to San Antonio, Texas. It was the last Civil War battle fought in New Mexico.

OTHER HISPANICS IN THE CIVIL WAR

Aside from those in the Southwest, a handful of Hispanics also took part in the Civil War in other parts of the United States. The Spanish legacy in Louisiana had not disappeared, as is shown by the existence of a Spanish regiment in the state militia. On the Union side, a group of Hispanic troops were in the 39th New York Regiment of Volunteers. It was nicknamed the Garibaldi Guard in honor of Giuseppe Garibaldi, an Italian patriot who at the same time was fighting to unify Italy. The regiment was recruited in New York City and was composed of three Hungarian companies, three German, one Swiss, one Italian, one French, one Portuguese, and one Spanish. The 39th fought from almost the beginning of the Civil War to its end, taking part in some of the most famous battles, including that at Gettysburg, Pennsylvania, a Union victory that turned back a Confederate invasion of the North, and the final campaign at Appomattox, Virginia, which forced the South to finally surrender.

It was at Gettysburg that Colonel Federico Fernández Cavada, born in Cuba, commanded a regiment of Pennsylvania troops. His 114th Pennsylvania Infantry fought Confederates at the bloody Peach Orchard area of the battle. However, he was captured in 1863 and held prisoner at Libby Prison for almost a year. Fernández Cavada was released from prison in 1864, and his book *Libby Life* denounced inhumane conditions at the prison. Fernández Cavada later joined the Cuban army in its battle for

LORETA JANETA VELÁZQUEZ

Perhaps the oddest story about a Hispanic in the Civil War is the tale of a Cuban-born woman named Loreta Janeta Velázquez, who dressed herself as a Confederate soldier and enlisted under the name Harry Buford. She fought at the battles of Bull Run, Ball's Bluff, and Fort Donelson, but her disguise was uncovered by a doctor treating her for a bullet wound. She became a spy for the South and wrote a book called *The Woman in Battle*, published in 1876.

independence from colonial Spain. He was captured in battle and executed in 1871 by Spanish authorities despite pleas for mercy from President Ulysses S. Grant and other Union generals under whom he had served.

A Confederate counterpart to Fernández Cavada was Ambrosio Gonzales, another Cuban, who fought in both the U.S. Civil War and, earlier, in Cuba's colonial wars against Spain. In 1850, Gonzales landed in Cuba as part of a failed expedition to end Spanish rule in Cuba. The mission had been financed by Southerners who wanted Cuba to enter the Union as a slave state, and Gonzales was involved in the negotiations between the Cubans and the Southerners. He remained interested in the Southern cause, and when the U.S. Civil War started, he joined the Confederate Army and rose to the rank of colonel. At the Battle of Honey Hill, Gonzales commanded the artillery of General P. G. T. Beauregard that helped win the fight for the South.

The most famous Hispanic in the Civil War was perhaps Admiral David G. Farragut, the son of a merchant seaman from the Spanish island of Minorca, who became the leading Union naval officer during the Civil War. In 1862, Farragut was in command of the Northern squadron of ships that ran past Confederate defenses and took the port and city of New Orleans, giving the Union control of the Mississippi River at its mouth on the Gulf of Mexico. The following year he did not fare as well in the sieges of Port Hudson and Vicksburg— the last major Confederate strongholds on the Mississippi

north of New Orleans—because of a failure to coordinate his ships with army forces on land.

But Farragut gained a great triumph in 1864 when he defeated a Confederate fleet at the Battle of Mobile Bay, which allowed the Union to occupy what had been the South's last port on the Gulf of Mexico.

That victory made Farragut a national hero, and after the war he was made the first full admiral of the U.S. Navy. He is perhaps best known today for the order he supposedly gave at Mobile, "Damn the torpedoes, full speed ahead!" Farragut was urging his men to disregard the danger of explosives, and charge on to victory. Although historians are in dispute about the exact words he used, the phrase remains a rallying cry for the U.S. Navy today.

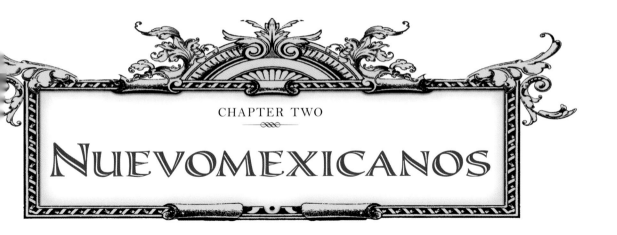

CHAPTER TWO

NUEVOMEXICANOS

A FTER THE END OF THE CIVIL WAR, IT WAS clear that New Mexico was different from the other lands conquered by the United States in 1848. By the time that New Mexico became a U.S. territory in 1850, it was home to 57,000 Hispanics and just 2,000 Anglos. Thirty years later, the Anglo population was about 10,000, while the Hispanics numbered close to 80,000, an eight-to-one ratio. In New Mexico, therefore, the Hispanic population was larger than in Texas or California.

But after 1850, the Hispanos of New Mexico continued to search for their identity, while feeling pressure to become more like the English-speaking outsiders moving in. At that point, the land where *Nuevomexicano* families had lived for generations, first under Spain and then under Mexico, had

Opposite: Hispanics tried to find their place among Anglos when New Mexico went from belonging to Mexico to belonging to the United States.

The upper class of New Mexico was made up of sheep farmers, whose ranches made fortunes for their owners.

been part of the United States for less than twenty years and had not yet become a full-fledged state like Texas or California. Hispanos asked themselves whether they were American, a separate Spanish-speaking people, or maybe a little of both. New Mexico also had its own entrenched upper class, called the *ricos*, or rich ones. These were Spanish-speaking families who had made small fortunes in sheep ranching.

The region the Hispanos lived in had passed from belonging to Mexico to belonging to the United States nineteen years earlier. That time period was long enough to become distinct from the old country, but not long enough to become fully like the new one. "No longer a 'Mexican' territory, yet still very unlike a typical American state, New Mexico exhibited a decidedly mixed character," historian Charles Montgomery wrote in *Spanish Redemption*.

"The colonial settlers from which most Hispanos . . . descended were the product of generations of unions among Spaniards (both *peninsulares*, those who were born in Spain and *criollos*, those whose parents were Iberian born), *mestizos*, *mulattoes* and New Mexico's Indian tribes."

LAND GRANT WARS

Many of the elite Hispanic families, as well as some poorer ones, could trace ownership of their land to the more than two hundred grants given to settlers in New Mexico by the king of Spain during colonial times. After the territory became part of the United States at the end of the Mexican War in 1848, the Treaty of Guadalupe Hidalgo was drawn up to protect land grants held by Hispanos. But the treaty did

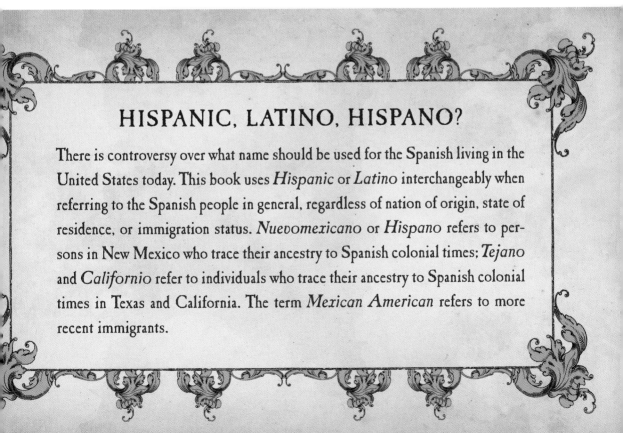

HISPANIC, LATINO, HISPANO?

There is controversy over what name should be used for the Spanish living in the United States today. This book uses *Hispanic* or *Latino* interchangeably when referring to the Spanish people in general, regardless of nation of origin, state of residence, or immigration status. *Nuevomexicano* or *Hispano* refers to persons in New Mexico who trace their ancestry to Spanish colonial times; *Tejano* and *Californio* refer to individuals who trace their ancestry to Spanish colonial times in Texas and California. The term *Mexican American* refers to more recent immigrants.

not hold up when wealthy Anglo *speculators* entered New Mexico and challenged the legitimacy of the grants. Hispanos had to hire lawyers to defend their titles of ownership and land surveyors to map the limits of their properties, then wait for the federal government back in Washington, D.C., to make a decision in each case.

The wealthiest families were able to afford these expenses, but many owners of small and medium-sized ranches could not. The poorer families gave up and sold their land to the outsiders. A related problem was that some of the old land grants were communal holdings, that is, they were owned by villages rather than individuals. This was traditional under Spanish law but not under the laws of the United States. In 1896, the Supreme Court issued a ruling stating that many of those communal lands were not owned by the villages but by the federal government. More than 6 million acres (2.4 million hectares) were set aside for national forests and homesteading. As Charles Montgomery wrote, that left many Hispanos "an agricultural plot barely large enough to grow a few bushels of corn."

Disagreements between Anglos and Hispanos over land rights sometimes turned violent. There were land grant wars throughout northern New Mexico in Colfax, San Miguel, and Lincoln counties. A secret group known as the Gorras Blancas (White Caps) burned down barns owned by Anglos who had taken Hispano land. They also tore down fencing they thought illegally divided the Hispano sheep ranchers' communal grazing lands that had afforded many Hispano sheep ranchers their livelihood.

THE POWER OF HISPANOS

Despite the land grant setbacks, New Mexico gradually became a center of Hispanic political power. As Stephen C. Martínez said in an essay published online by the University of New Mexico, "Nuevomexicanos established an important and lasting culture of civic participation which is unmatched by any Latino group in the history of the U.S." During the second half of the nineteenth century, more than three-quarters of the members of the Territorial Legislature (where laws were made before New Mexico became a state), were Hispanic, as were nine delegates to the U.S. Congress. Over the last third of that century, prominent Anglo and Hispano families sometimes competed in politics, sometimes cooperated in civil affairs, and sometimes even intermarried.

Still, the influx of eastern businessmen slowly took power away from the Hispano elite, athough neither side could gain complete control. Rafael Chacón, who was a soldier, businessman, rancher, and politician, lived through and helped shape many of these changes. He was born in 1833, when New Mexico was still a part of Mexico, and died in 1925, after New Mexico had become the forty-seventh state. Chacón attended a Mexican military academy and fought against the U.S. Army when it attacked Santa Fe during the

Mexican War. But as time went on, he began to feel less like a Mexican soldier and more like an American. He even became a captain in the Union army during the U.S. Civil War, commanding a company at the Battle of Glorieta Pass when Hispano soldiers slipped behind Confederate lines to destroy supplies and force a retreat.

He wasn't always rewarded for his services. New Mexican historian Enrique Lamadrid wrote, "As captain of a company of Hispano volunteers who defended the Union cause at the battles of Valverde and Glorieta . . . he spent his personal fortune on horses for his men, expenses that the United States Army promised to reimburse, but never did."

Captain Rafael Chacón wrote his memoirs while he was in his seventies, in order to record the drama, adventure, and sorrow he experienced during his lifetime.

After his military career, Chacón served several terms in the Territorial Legislature, where he dealt with issues of statehood and land ownership. He left politics and became a rancher. His *Memorias*, an autobiography, was published in 1991 by the University of New Mexico Press and remains a valuable resource about Hispanic life in the mid- to late-nineteenth century.

Another important Hispano leader was Civil War veteran José Francisco Chaves, who came from a wealthy family long prominent in New Mexico politics—his grandfather had been governor of New Mexico after Mexico achieved independence from Spain in 1821. Chaves studied medicine in New York City, but returned to New Mexico to become a cattle rancher. He joined the Union Army during the Civil War and fought at the Battle of Valverde in 1862, won by the Confederacy. Nevertheless, he gained promotion to lieutenant colonel for "gallant and meritorious service." After the war ended, he became the leader of the Republican Party in New Mexico. From 1865 to 1871, he served as a delegate in Washington, D.C., but like the other men who represented New Mexico, he did not have a vote because New Mexico was not yet a state. Chaves worked to convince Congress to grant New Mexico statehood. To not do so, he said, was "incompatible with the principles of a republican system." In 1904, he was killed by an unknown assassin, eight years before New Mexico became the forty-seventh state.

After serving for a number of years as a delegate in the U.S. House of Representatives, José Francisco Chaves worked as a rancher who raised livestock.

CAMPAIGNING FOR STATEHOOD

Sixty-two years passed between 1850, when New Mexico officially became a territory, and, 1912, the year that Congress finally awarded it statehood. Why did it take so long? The last third of the nineteenth century was a time of distrust people unlike the dominant Anglo Protestant culture, whether they were the millions of European Roman Catholic and Jewish immigrants pouring into the country, or the Catholic Hispanic New Mexicans. But there was another element that made some Americans question Hispanic loyalty. Immigrants to the United States had traveled there for a better life, but Nuevomexicanos were a conquered people—they had not come to the United States, the United States had come to them.

As a result, the Hispanos of New Mexico spent decades trying to make New Mexico a state while remaining true to their culture. Some of the leading Anglo residents such as Max Frost, editor of the *New Mexican* newspaper and Governor L. Bradford Prince, elected in 1888, helped the statehood cause because they believed everyone in New Mexico would benefit if the territory became a state and gained voting representatives in Congress. The campaign became stronger in the 1870s and 1880s, led by the Santa Fe Ring, a group of Anglo and Nuevomexicano lawyers, politicians, and landowners. Thanks mostly to the work of the Santa Fe Ring, in 1874, the Territorial Legislature unanimously passed a resolution asking Congress to give New Mexico statehood. The lawmakers, aware of the cultural *xenophobia*, or fear of foreigners, of the times, made a point of saying that New Mexico's population was predominantly Caucasian "of European and American descent" except for peaceful Native Americans such as the Pueblo tribes. Hispanos, who at least in part descended from European Spaniards, included themselves as part of that Caucasian population. The document did not say much about New Mexico's unique blend of Hispanic, Anglo, and Native American cultures. One response was an openly racist congressional report that painted Nuevomexicanos as mixed-blooded and inferior. "Of the native population but few are pure blood or Castilian," the report said. The rest, it went on, lived in "ignorance, superstition and sloth." In 1876, Congress voted down the statehood proposal. Between 1888 and 1895, proposals failed at least five more times.

The proud people of New Mexico did not let the insults stand unchallenged. In 1890, Antonio Joseph, born of Hispano and Anglo parents, wrote in the Santa Fe Spanish-language newspaper *La Voz del Pueblo, The Voice of the People*, "It is not by blood or language that one measures the devotion of New Mexico's people to the United States and its institutions." He went on to say that Nuevomexicanos were "descendants of the daring discoverers who abandoned the *monarchial* institutions of Spain and moved to the New World . . . to break away from foreign domination."

Some historians believe a key reason why New Mexico became a state was that Hispanos defined themselves (and were seen by some outsiders) as being of European Spanish descent, not as mixed-blood Mexicans. Even Spanish descent

was no guarantee of acceptance. During the Spanish-American War of 1898 (during which the United States defeated Spain to take control of former Spanish colonies Cuba, Puerto Rico, and the Philippines), rumors abounded that the Hispanos of New Mexico secretly sympathized with Spain. But New Mexico's chief justice, Lebaron Bradford Prince, said at a *congressional hearing* for statehood that "no less than 1,089 volunteers" from New Mexico had enlisted for the war, some 500 of whom were in Teddy Roosevelt's famous Rough Riders, a cavalry regiment that included Americans from such diverse backgrounds as college athletes and frontiersmen. Roosevelt led the charge up San Juan Hill in Cuba, a decisive land battle of the war. Roosevelt's success brought him so much popularity he was elected vice president in 1900 and became president in 1901 when William McKinley was assassinated. Roosevelt was reelected president in 1904.

The pro-statehood forces eventually won. They were helped by President William Howard Taft, who in 1910 authorized New Mexico to write a new constitution in preparation to being admitted as a state. The document was approved by New Mexico voters in 1911, and the following year, President Taft signed the law that made the territory the forty-seventh state of the United States. Taft believed the people of New Mexico, Anglo or Hispano, were entitled to statehood, and also thought that making New Mexico a state would gain votes for his Republican Party. Taft's words at the signing were, "I am glad to give you life, I hope that you will be healthy."

CHAPTER THREE

Tejanos

LIKE NEW MEXICO, TEXAS WAS ONCE PART OF
the Spanish empire, and then part of Mexico. Texas
broke away from Mexico in 1836, and in 1845 it was
annexed by the United States. That action began the United
States-Mexico War. During the nine years Texas was not part
of Mexico or of the United States. It was a *sovereign nation*
recognized diplomatically by international powers like Great
Britain and France. Over those years of independence, the
Republic of Texas was governed by Anglo settlers who had
migrated to Texas in the preceding years. In fact, so many
Anglo-American settlers moved in that they outnumbered
the old-time Hispanic inhabitants even while the territory
belonged to Mexico.

Opposite:
A young
Hispanic boy.

Less than two decades after its annexation to the Union, Texas left the Union to join the Confederate States of America in the Civil War. After the end of the war, Tejanos, like the Nuevomexicanos, spent much time trying to figure out who they were—how to be American while keeping the Spanish language, the Catholic religion, and some of their Spanish and Mexican cultural traditions. Still, as historian Arnoldo De León wrote in *The Tejano Community, 1836-1900*, even though "racism and oppression made the great majority of [Tejanos] politically powerless and financially poor," the two communities came together in some ways, so that "a matured Mexican culture evolved into one that was simultaneously both American and Texan."

Tejanos continued to eat beans, tamales, and tortillas, not because they had no other choice, but because they found traditional Mexican food familiar and delicious. But not everyone was so content. De León wrote that there were those who "sought to marry Anglos because they believed that marriage ties would elevate their social status." Still, *biculturalism* in those years was not like it is among Mexican Americans today—back then there were Hispanic ethnic activists who were also white supremacists. For instance, a prominent politician named José Antonio Navarro led the fight against the Know-Nothing party, which was created to oppose immigrants and Catholics, and fought for the voting rights of Spanish-speakers. Yet he was also active in white racist causes. Navarro supported the Confederacy after the

Civil War ended and, as De León wrote, "emerged as a leading Caucasian supremacist in the San Antonio area."

POLITICAL PARTICIPATION

José Antonio Navarro was not the only Hispanic in Texas to oppose the right of African Americans. During the *Reconstruction* years after the war, Navarro and other Caucasian Tejanos, who descended mostly from early Spanish settlers, formed an organization called *Los Bexareños Demócratas* (The Bexar Democrats, Bexar being a county in Texas) that held protest rallies—in Spanish—to oppose the efforts of Republicans to bring equal rights to the newly *emancipated* African Americans. A rival group, the Mexican-Texan Club, also held meetings in Spanish and even had its own Spanish-language newspaper, *El Mexicano de Texas*, but favored racial equality between African Americans and Caucasians. These divisions among Tejanos reflected the bitterly split American nation of the post-Civil War period. In some parts of Texas, Democrats were nicknamed *guaraches*, the lower class, and

José Antonio Navarro championed the independence of Texas from Mexico and fought for the rights of Tejanos.

Republicans *botas*, the wealthy class. The fact that one Tejano group could be pro-slavery and the other pro-equality, and that both mounted their campaigns in Spanish and were affiliated with the major national political parties of the day, shows to what extent Tejanos had become American.

Political participation by Hispanics in Texas continued throughout the 1870s and into the 1880s. Tejanos were active in presidential politics. In the 1872 election, there were Democratic organizations that supported candidate Horace Greeley, and others that backed the eventual winner, Republican Ulysses S. Grant. In heavily Hispanic regions such as San Antonio and El Paso, dozens of men with Spanish surnames like Quintana, Nuñez, and Chávez were elected to municipal and county offices. The town of Laredo had five Hispanic mayors from 1877 to 1884. All this gave the Hispanic community some political power. When Tejanos were banned from dancing at San Pedro Park in San Antonio in 1883, Hispanic politicians organized protest rallies and threatened to bring a lawsuit. They regained the right to dance. Tejanos continued to hold office in significant numbers until the 1890s, when the Anglo population topped the Hispanic population even in much of south Texas.

While Hispanics were gaining some control, Anglos held more political power. One reason for this was that even in areas where the Hispanic population was larger than the Anglo, more Anglos than Hispanics were qualified to vote. For instance, historian De León found that in El Paso County in 1860, there were 912 Tejano males of voting age and 318 Anglo males of voting age (women were not allowed to vote then)—but once U.S. citizenship and literacy were taken into account, there were 159 Anglos eligible to vote and just 149 Tejanos. Many Tejanos were not U.S. citizens or could not pass the literacy tests then required of voters.

A typical vaquero from the 1800s.

RACISM

Another problem Tejanos faced was prejudice stemming from anti-Catholic feelings and racial issues. "Caucasians, who outnumbered the native Tejanos by ten to one in 1836, were not about to countenance being ruled indefinitely by a people who in their view resembled Negroes and Indians," De León wrote. Tejanos were shut out of good jobs, or they were paid less than Anglos for doing the same work.

Tejanos had for generations tended sheep and cattle, and refined the riding and roping techniques their ancestors had brought from Spain. These *pastores* (shepherds) and *vaqueros* (cowboys) earned the respect of

Anglos. "They are better suited to this business than any other race in existence," wrote one observer in the late 1850s, as quoted by De León. These Tejanos maintained their reputation, and their jobs, into the 1880s. But by the end of the century, Anglos had "spread . . . into the rural scene, displacing Tejanos," as De León wrote. Many Tejanos were forced to take much less prestigious jobs picking cotton or food crops.

A Tejano drives a water cart in Texas in the 1850s.

Some Tejanos moved to the cities. But there, Anglos were more likely to work in the higher-paying professions

and in skilled crafts such as carpentry, while Tejanos were more likely to be laborers and servants. One study showed that in the middle of the nineteenth century, about half of the Anglos in Texas owned property worth above $1,000, compared with just 16.1 percent of Tejanos. As late as the end of that century, 43 percent of young Tejanos in five south Texas counties were employed as common laborers, compared with 19 percent of young Anglos.

There was also racially motivated violence. In the years after the Civil War, Mexican cattle thieves staged raids, and Anglo ranchers countered with armed *posses* that captured and lynched alleged bandits. Sometimes they hung the wrong person. De León quotes an American diplomat in Mexico, who "testified that Caucasian authorities disregarded aggressions upon Mexicanos and that . . . no one made a great fuss over the hanging or killing of a Mexican."

Everyday Life

Despite the backdrop of violence in the Tejano communities, life went on in the towns, in the cities, and on the ranches. Some rural folk lived in traditional dwellings called *jacals*, log cabins. These homes were built using posts and logs from the mesquite tree. Roof thatching was made by tying together strips of a South Texas yucca plant called the *pita*. During winters, families kept out wind and cold by filling crevices between logs with insulation made from limestone and corn husks. A sturdier kind of ranch home, made of blocks of limestone, was known as a *sillar*.

A typical ranch of those years was founded by José Antonio López and his wife, María de los Santos González, who arrived in south Texas from Mexico in late 1869 and whose life was recounted years later by a descendant, Andrés Sáenz. Like other ranchers on the dry, near-desert land, one of the first things Antonio López had to do to make his land livable was to find a source of drinking water. On his first try, he dug 35 feet (10.7 meters) into the hard, dry ground but struck only salty water. Luckily, he found fresh water on his second try. The daily work of getting the water, however, was much more difficult than merely turning on a faucet as we do today. "It took two people to draw water from the well," Sáenz wrote, "one person on horseback pulled the bucket out of the water, and another emptied the water into the troughs for watering the sheep, goats, and cattle." By 1886, Antonio López owned 640 acres (259 hectares) of land, forty mares, twenty fillies, seven saddle horses, seven colts, forty-eight cows, and eight yearlings.

Meanwhile, in the cities, one common characteristic of Tejano society was the *mutualista* organizations, or mutual aid societies. "They offered members burial and illness benefits, legal aid and emergency loans . . . established newspapers, libraries and private (mostly primary) schools . . . sponsored dances, patriotic and anniversary celebrations," Cynthia Orozco wrote in *Mexican Americans in Texas History*. "They also promoted participation in the political process by fielding and endorsing candidates, supporting specific campaigns, and urging Mexican nationals to legalize their status to become voters."

Tejanos and Tejano culture survived. Today, the descendants of those Tejano pioneers still make up part of the Hispanic population of Texas and have full rights as U.S. citizens. They live alongside immigrants who arrived more recently from Mexico and other parts of Latin America.

CHAPTER FOUR

CALIFORNIOS

LTHOUGH TEXAS WAS AN INDEPENDENT country for nine years, the Republic of California lasted just one month. Like Texas, California had been part of the Spanish empire and then part of Mexico. But then a band of American settlers, led by military officer John C. Frémont, took over the headquarters of Mexican General Mariano Vallejo in Sonoma in 1846. The Americans, who had heard that the United States and Mexico were at war, proclaimed the independence of the Republic of California. They raised their Bear Flag, which they had created to show California's independence. That July, Commodore John Sloat landed at Monterey with an American warship and claimed possession of California for the United States. The Republic of California had lasted only one month. The California territory was admitted to the Union as a state in 1850.

Opposite: Americans taking over General Vallejo's headquarters, under the Bear Flag of the California Republic.

The Bear Flag that Frémont designed for California can still be seen on the modern-day state flag, and residents and visitors alike can still enjoy the twenty-one missions built there by the Spanish between 1769 and 1823. But the *Californios*, as the Spanish-speaking people of the region were then called, had by the end of the nineteenth century practically disappeared from history. Some of them assimilated into the growing Anglo population, others blended with the population of new immigrants from Mexico.

In the first few years of California statehood, however, it did not seem that the Hispanic culture was about to die. Many Spanish speakers adjusted to life as U.S. citizens. Vallejo was one of eight Californio delegates, out of forty-eight in total, elected to the constitutional convention in 1849—"a generous representation," wrote historian Leonard Pitt in *The Decline of the Californios*, "considering that the number of Californios did not exceed 13,000 total in a population of 100,000." To pave the way for admission to the Union, the Californios joined in a unanimous vote to ban slavery—the most controversial issue of the time. Delegates also agreed to the eight Californios' demand that all state laws and regulations be published also in Spanish.

INFLUENCE OF SPANISH SPEAKERS

Although there was tension between Hispanics and Anglos throughout the first decade of California's life as a state and into the Civil War, Californios worked hard to gain political

influence and retain their cultural traditions. Even as the Anglo population increased in the 1870s and 1880s, Californio community life continued to flourish. Californios held bullfights and rodeos, and observed traditions from the old country such as the celebration of Mexican Independence Day.

In political life, "A prestigious Spanish surname (especially when combined with a Caucasian face) remained a good entrée into public office," Pitt noted. Several Californios were elected to the state assembly, and Romualdo Pacheco even became a U.S. Congressman. Pacheco was a highly influential Californio. He had served as a Union officer in the Civil War, and in 1869 aided Mexican president Benito Juárez raise funds in California to help Mexico fight the French forces who were occupying the country (the French tried to take over Mexico after it declared it could not afford to pay debts it owed foreign countries). Pacheco was also the first and only Hispanic governor of California; he was elected lieutenant governor in 1871, and stepped up to the higher office in 1875.

Political developments were reported by Spanish-language newspapers like *La Voz de Méjico* (*The Voice of Mexico*) in San Francisco and *La Crónica* (*The Chronicle*) in Los Angeles in the 1870s. The Spanish-speaking population was considered important enough for the *Los Angeles Times* and *San Francisco Herald* to print Spanish-language sheets at election time. It was not uncommon for Caucasian Californios to marry Anglos. For instance, two daughters of Mariano Vallejo, the grand old patriarch of Californios, married brothers by the last name of Frisbie, and Vallejo's son, Platón, went to medical school in New York and married a non-Hispanic Caucasian woman from Syracuse. Racism against Hispanics was not as strong as it was against blacks during the era.

But the fortunes of the Vallejo family began to sink. Like many other Hispanics in the territory that had once been part of Mexico, Vallejo found that ownership of his land was being challenged by outsiders. Although the Treaty of Guadalupe Hidalgo recognized the rights of Hispanic landowners now in U.S. territory, Vallejo had to pay thousands of dollars in legal fees to prove the land belonged to him. The expenses grew so high that in order to pay the lawyers, Vallejo had to sell off the very land he was paying the lawyers to defend. By the time he died in 1890, all that was left of the quarter million acres (101,171 ha) he once owned was the modest 200-acre (81-ha) ranch he called *Lachryma Montis*, Latin for *Tear of the Mountain*.

INFLUENCE LOST

Most Californios found themselves in the same predicament as Mariano Vallejo, losing their lands to Anglos through a combination of unfair laws and economic pressure. The beginning of the decline of Californios can be traced back to the late 1840s. The United States-Mexico War had barely ended when a major influx of Anglos entered the California territory after the 1848 discovery of gold. By the following year the California gold rush, which brought people from all over the world to California in search of gold, was in full swing.

Soon there were more Anglos than Californios, leaving the latter culturally outnumbered and outvoted when it came to politics. It is estimated that Californios made up just 4 percent of the state's population by 1870. At first, the greatest Anglo population growth was in northern California due to the gold rush. Southern California remained more Hispanic. However, in the late 1870s and early 1880s, the building of the transcontinental railroad brought another explosion in the Anglo population. Trains arrived in Los Angeles, dropping off more than 120,000 passengers in 1887. By then,

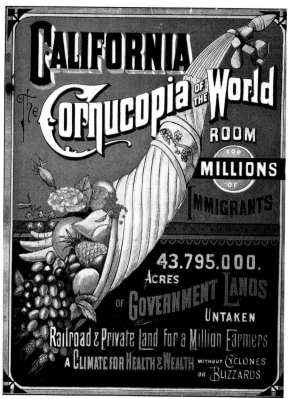

In order to make moving to California more appealing, The American Land Company created a poster boasting of reasons to move to the area.

Anglos also outnumbered Hispanics in the southern part of the state. That year, historian Pitt estimates, there were about 12,000 Hispanics in Los Angeles, counting old-line Californios and newer immigrants from Mexico, but that number amounted to less than 10 percent of the population. "The types of consumer goods advertised for sale, the tastes in food and dress, the prevalence of Great Britain over Spanish in daily and official conversation . . . all changed rapidly and irreversibly," Pitt wrote. The newcomers set off a land boom, and the process of breaking up old ranchos into small farms and towns was sped up.

COPING WITH LOSS

Without the land upon which family fortunes had depended for generations, Californios lost political and economic power. But they never lost their pride. Groups of forty or fifty men who had lost their lands would travel in all their finery from one sheep ranch to another looking for work. They wore "silver-trimmed bridles and stirrups, tooled leather

BANDIDOS OR HEROES?

In reaction to the racism the Spanish people felt in nineteenth-century California, some Spanish speakers turned to what neutral historians have called social banditry. Others are less neutral. To Spanish supporters, men like Tiburcio Vásquez and Joaquin Murrieta were Hispanic heroes who stood up to Anglo domination. To others, they were common criminals.

Murrieta was active during the gold rush in the 1850s. Legend says that racism prevented him from making a legal living, so he started a gang called The Five Joaquins that was responsible for most of the cattle rustling and killings in the Sierra Nevada at that time. In 1853, a group of lawmen allegedly killed him in a shootout. A human head that was said to be Murrieta's, preserved in a jar with alcohol, was displayed throughout California. A woman who claimed she was his sister insisted it was not Murrieta's head.

Vásquez became famous in some parts of California after he and his band killed three men and stole two hundred dollars in San Benito County in 1873. After a year-long crime spree, he was captured, tried, and sentenced to death by hanging.

Vásquez tried to justify himself by claiming he had been discriminated against and that his actions might return California to Mexico. But California governor Romualdo Pacheco refused to grant clemency. Vásquez was executed in 1875.

WANTED!

EL TEATRO CAMPESINO
presents

BANDIDO!

The American Melodrama of
TIBURCIO VASQUEZ
Notorious California Bandit
written and directed by
LUIS VALDEZ

A vaquero dressed in his finest.

saddles, broadcloth suits, ruffled shirts, dark sombreros," Leonard Pitt wrote. But ranch work was seasonal, lasting only for three to eight months each year, and even though the men had much experience as vaqueros or shepherds, Anglos held most of the supervisory positions.

Other Californios moved to the cities to work as laborers in railroad, construction, and food processing. Hostility from Anglos and low levels of education formed barriers to upward mobility. Even in such skilled blue-collar positions as hatmaker, mason, and tailor, there were few Hispanics. It was while working as laborers that Californios more and more frequently encountered other Spanish speakers— immigrants who were then coming from Mexico, mostly from poverty-stricken backgrounds.

The two groups had cultural similarities, but there were also differences. For example, Californios tended to live in large families, while the new immigrants were often single men who lived in boardinghouses. In addition, the newcomers were almost all working class, but some of the Californios dispossessed of their lands had managed to get an education and work in higher-paying professions, living as Spanish Americans next to Anglo neighbors in new sections of cities such as Los Angeles. Intermarriage at that time was fairly common, sometimes between a Californio and Anglo, often between a Californio and Mexican immigrant.

The rate of intermarriage and increased immigration from Mexico to California meant that by the early 1900s the number of people who identified themselves as Mexican or Mexican American was larger than the number of those who saw themselves as descendants of the Californio aristocracy. The old Californio culture was in its dying days. The Hispanic legacy in California, as in the rest of the United States, would be revived in decades to come by the millions of immigrants who made their way to the United States from every corner of the Spanish-speaking world, looking for the economic opportunities or the basic freedoms they could not find in their countries of origin.

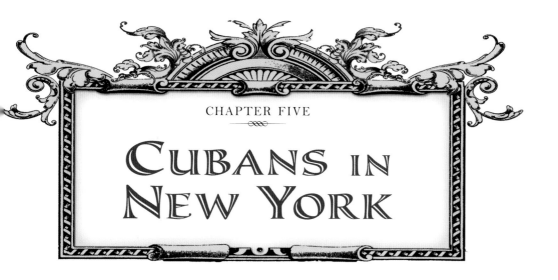

CHAPTER FIVE

CUBANS IN NEW YORK

O
NE OF THE MOST COMMON IMAGES OF nineteenth-century New York immigrants is that of the European, perhaps one of the Irish who began to emigrate in the 1830s, or one of the Italians and Jews who, some decades later, arrived by the millions. Cubans also migrated to New York beginning in the 1830s and on through the end of the century. There was never a large enough population, however, to leave an unmistakable imprint on the city the way European immigrants did. But New York's Cubans had a disproportionate impact on the history of Cuba itself, because much of the fund-raising and organizing for Cuba's struggle for independence from Spain took place in New York from the 1830s to the 1890s.

Opposite: A large number of people left their home countries in the 1800s to immigrate to America.

49

The first well-known Cuban to immigrate to New York was a Catholic priest named Félix Varela. In Cuba in 1821, Varela was elected to represent his country in a new, democratic-leaning Spanish parliament. But in 1823, parliament was dissolved by the *absolutist king* Ferdinand VII of Spain, and Varela fled to New York.

For the first few years after he arrived, Varela continued to work for the independence of Cuba. He founded *El Habañero, The Havanan*, one of the first Spanish-language newspapers in the United States. The paper was smuggled to Cuba, where it was read by conspirators plotting to free the island from Spanish rule.

In New York, meanwhile, the Cuban community was politically divided. There were *independentistas*, or independentists, who wanted Cuba to be a sovereign republic. More timid were the *autonomistas*, or autonomists, who sought increased self-rule for Cuba but as a province under the Spanish crown. And there were *anexionistas*, annexionists who wanted Cuba to become part of the United States. The anexionistas were divided in two camps: those who wanted Cuba to join the Union as a state that permitted slavery, and those who sought American democracy and wanted to abolish slavery. Varela was so admired by other Cubans that he brought together rivals like autonomista José Antonio Saco and anexionista Gaspar Betancourt Cisneros to discuss the pressing Cuban issues of the day.

There were so many divisions, however, and so little support from the United States and Latin American governments, that Valera realized Cuban independence was far off. So he concentrated on his priestly duties. In 1832, Father Valera founded the School of the Transfiguration of Our Lord in New York City. Most of the students were the children of desperately poor Irish immigrants.

That summer, there was a cholera epidemic in New York. Contemporary accounts tell of uncollected rubbish, of sick men and unburied corpses lying in gutters. Mortality was highest in the Irish slum known as Five Points. And it

A number of Irish immigrants lived in an area called Five Points in the Lower East Side of New York City.

was there—where some doctors refused to set foot— that Varela tended to the sick and risked his own life. He became a beloved figure, known by the people as the Vicar of the Irish. For the next decade and a half, Varela continued to help Catholic immigrants until 1848, when he retired to Saint Augustine, Florida, where he had lived as a child when it belonged to Spain. He died five years later.

PLOTTING WARS

Politics remained an important part of life in New York's small Cuban community after Varela's death. With Manifest Destiny in the air after the defeat of Mexico in 1848, and with tensions rising between northern and southern states, some Americans became interested in anexionista proposals to let Cuba join the Union as a slave state. One activist, Venezuela-born Narciso López, traveled between New York, Washington, D.C., and New Orleans to organize an invasion of Cuba sponsored by anexionistas and pro-slavery Southerners.

One plot failed in 1849 when the U.S. Navy blockaded eight hundred of López's followers off the coast of Mississippi. The next year, he led six hundred armed men from Florida to Cuba. They landed before sunrise in Cárdenas, on the northern coast of the island, and raised the Cuban flag for the first time on Cuban soil. But when Spanish troops counterattacked, López retreated to Florida. He organized yet another expedition to Cuba in

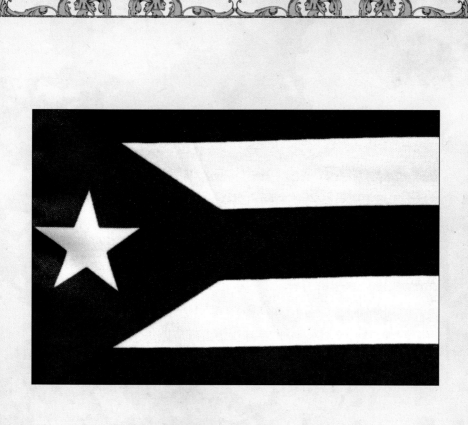

NEW YORK'S CUBAN FLAG

The flag that flew over Cárdenas during Narciso López's brief occupation, and which became the official flag of the Republic of Cuba, was created in New York City in 1849. According to Cuban legend, one summer day as he plotted the invasion of Cuba, López noted the blue sky and white clouds above Manhattan, which inspired a vision for a flag his expedition would carry. López later added the red triangle with the lone white star.

1851, but he was captured and executed by Spanish authorities.

In the fifteen years following the death of Narciso López, Cubans in the United States launched more armed expeditions in Cuba, but those were also stopped by the Spanish colonial government. Then, in 1868, Cubans led by Carlos Manuel de Céspedes, a landowner who had freed his slaves, launched a major rebellion in Cuba against Spanish rule. It lasted a decade and has become known as the Ten Years' War. Thousands of Cubans sought refuge in the United States. The Census of 1870 found 1,565 Cuban-born persons in New York City alone; there were probably even more in the following few years, at the height of the Ten Years' War.

Carlos Manuel de Céspedes freed his slaves and brought them into his armed force.

Such a high concentration of Cubans in New York gave rise to a small Cuban district in downtown Manhattan. There were dozens of Cuban-owned cigar factories on Pearl Street and Maiden Lane, and other types of businesses arose to cater to the Cubans' needs.

Other immigrants were wealthy Havana merchants who tried to help the rebels in Cuba. José Morales Lemus, head of the Junta Central Republicana de Cuba y Puerto Rico, a

Cuban revolutionary club in New York, tried to convince the United States to recognize Cuban independence, but was not successful. Other New York Cubans took a more direct approach, and in 1873, they sent a ship named the *Virginius* full of supplies for the rebels. The ship was captured by Spanish authorities. Because there were American citizens among the crew, the incident almost sparked a war between the United States and Spain.

José Martí in New York

When the Ten Years' War ended in 1878, Cuba remained a Spanish colony. Another short-lived insurrection, known as the *Guerra Chiquita*, or Small War, took place the following

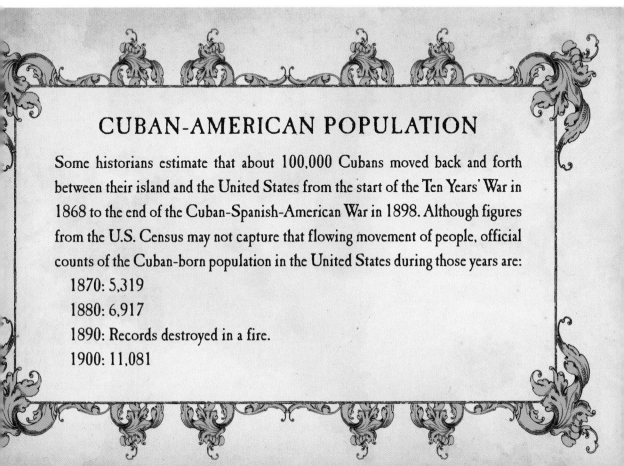

CUBAN-AMERICAN POPULATION

Some historians estimate that about 100,000 Cubans moved back and forth between their island and the United States from the start of the Ten Years' War in 1868 to the end of the Cuban-Spanish-American War in 1898. Although figures from the U.S. Census may not capture that flowing movement of people, official counts of the Cuban-born population in the United States during those years are:

1870: 5,319
1880: 6,917
1890: Records destroyed in a fire.
1900: 11,081

Cuban
independence
fighter
José Martí.

year. Cubans were so exhausted after a decade of fighting that few took up arms, so that effort to make Cuba independent also failed. One of its leaders escaped to New York. He was José Martí, who is considered the father of the Cuban nation in the same way that George Washington is called the father of the United States. Martí spent much of the 1880s in New York, trying to organize yet another rebellion in Cuba. But he was young (Martí had been only fifteen years old when the Ten Years' War started), and had no experience fighting, because during the short months that the Small War lasted, he had been in exile in Spain. For those reasons, the veterans of the Ten Years' War did not trust him.

Cuban generals Máximo Gómez and Antonio Maceo finally agreed to meet with the young Martí at a New York hotel in 1884. Gómez believed that during wartime, at least, the military should have the last word, so they clashed.

Martí biographer Jorge Mañach wrote that Gómez had been preparing for a bath when Martí arrived at the hotel. Gómez told Martí to leave New York and organize exiles in Mexico City. Martí agreed and spoke excitedly of plotting a revolution from there, but Gómez interrupted him. "Limit yourself to follow instructions," Mañach quotes him as saying. "As for anything else, attend to what Gen. Maceo may dispose." Then he stepped into his steam bath, ignoring Martí. Martí left the hotel knowing the encounter had been a disaster. Gómez went back to his home in the Dominican Republic and Maceo returned to his farm in Costa Rica. "Martí later wrote to Gómez, 'One cannot found a nation, General, the way one commands an army camp.'"

Although there was not much revolutionary activity among New York's Cubans for the next two years, the community continued to grow. By 1890, the U.S. Census counted 3,448 people from the Caribbean now in New York—a majority of whom were almost certainly Cuban. More businesses opened in the cigar-making neighborhoods downtown.

By 1890, Martí was again trying to bring together the young revolutionaries of his generation with veterans such as Gómez and Maceo. He gave patriotic speeches to crowds of Cubans in New York. "The voice came from the middle of the crowd but I could not see who it was," recalled one listener cited in Carlos Márquez Sterling's *Biografía de José Martí*. "A tenor-baritone, a warm and emotive voice that seemed to come from the heart without passing the lips . . . when he finished, a unanimous applause and a roar of enthusiasm . . . my friends ran over to me waving their arms, 'Come, come, it's Martí!'"

Martí was also a celebrated writer and poet. Visiting Latin American intellectuals would pay tribute to the famous man in his headquarters at 120 Front Street, and find themselves next to cigar factory workers from around the corner—they had all come to hear Martí speak.

It was the contributions of New York cigar workers that helped fund *Patria*, a newspaper Martí published to inform New York's Hispanic community and promote the independence of Cuba and Puerto Rico. But New York's Cubans alone would not be enough to help Cuba win the struggle for independence. By the late 1880s, Martí realized he would have to include the booming Cuban communities in Tampa and Key West in Florida.

FLORIDA REVOLUTIONARIES

F LORIDA REMAINED A SPANISH POSSESSION for more years than even New Mexico, which is considered the most Hispanic region of the Southwest. The first permanent European settlement in what is now the United States was Saint Augustine, Florida, founded by the Spanish in 1565. The first settlement in New Mexico did not come until 1598. New Mexico retained a Spanish colonial flavor, while Florida's Spanish colonial heritage mostly disappeared after the United States bought the territory from Spain in 1821.

All signs of Spanish heritage in Florida were not wiped out, however. For instance, the San Marcos Castle in Saint Augustine remains standing. A handful of Spanish Floridians

Opposite:
The waterfront of the city of Saint Augustine, Florida, founded in 1565, still thrives today.

made the transition, too, including Joseph Marion Hernández, who was born in Saint Augustine when it was still a Spanish colony and became Florida's delegate in Washington in 1822. Still, those are exceptions. Most of what is Hispanic in Florida today has its roots in the period after Spain left.

EARLY KEY WEST

Cuban immigration to Florida began in the 1830s, when Cuban cigar makers started working in Key West. Another influx came at the start of the Ten Years' War, when Cubans migrated to Key West fleeing political repression. Scholars estimate that by the end of the war in 1878, there were between seven and ten thousand Cubans in Key West, which was then an island reachable only by ship.

1. U. S. Military Cantonment.   2. Warehouses and Wharf of F. A. Browne.   3. Warehouses and Wharf of P. C. Greene.   4. Warehouses and Wharf of O. O'Hara.   5. Duval Street.   6. Front Street.   7. Fire Engine House.   8, Fleeming's Key and Naval Anchorage.   9. Turtle, Crab and Fish Market.   10. Blacksmiths Shop.   11. Tops of Cocoa Nuts North of the Warehouse.

THE BUSINESS PART OF
KEY-WEST.
Looking North.   Reduced from a pencil sketch by W. A. Whitehead Taken from the Cupola of the Warehouse of Messrs. A. C. Tift & Co.,   June 1838.

Key West was more of a working-class community than its counterpart in New York, but in Key West, Cubans accumulated more political power. Carlos Manuel de Céspedes, son of the rebel leader of the same name, became mayor in 1875, and in the 1880s Fernando Figueredo and Manuel Patricio Delgado were elected to Florida's state assembly. Florida's first Spanish-language newspaper, *El Yara* (named for the town in Cuba where a revolt took place that sparked the Ten Years' War) soon had a dozen competitors. There were Cuban doctors, hotel owners, restaurants, and coffee shops. By the mid-1870s, some 45 cigar factories employed 1,400 workers who made 25 million cigars a year. Cubans also founded the San Carlos Institute, an organization to preserve Cuban arts and culture, which still exists. Caucasian and African-American Cubans attended bilingual classes at San Carlos, making it one of the first racially integrated schools of the postwar South. José Martí spoke there in the early 1890s to unite Cubans in the struggle for independence. The original San Carlos building was knocked down by a hurricane in 1919; the structure that stands today, which was built in 1924 and renovated in 1992, remains a center of Cuban culture.

EARLY TAMPA

One of the cigar makers who settled in Key West at the beginning of the Ten Years' War was Vicente Martínez Ybor, a Spaniard who favored Cuban independence. He eventually grew unhappy with labor disputes there and the difficulties of transportation and providing water to Key West. So he bought land in a swamp near Tampa. He wanted not just to open a new factory but also to build subsidized housing for workers—a company town. It was the birth of Ybor City, Tampa's Cuban neighborhood.

An account of its early days, reported by Gary R. Mormino and George E. Pozzetta in *The Immigrant World of Ybor City,* tells of swarms of insects that forced residents "to go around with goggles to keep the gnats from their eyes." But the factory was

The Martínez Ybor cigar factory built in the 1800s still stands today and has been converted into a shopping and restaurant complex in Ybor City, Florida.

so successful, and the workers' homes that Martínez Ybor had built, starting in 1886, were so popular that more Cubans moved to the neighborhood. By 1895, Ybor City had 120 factories with some 5,000 workers. The 1900 census counted 1,313 native-born Cubans in Tampa, and 233 Spaniards, but there were probably many more. One newspaper editorial quoted by Mormino and Pozzetta said that "practically no count was made of the Spanish [-speaking] residents."

At a time of tension between Spaniards who wanted Spain to

BEATING YELLOW FEVER

The tropical disease known as yellow fever caused abdominal pain, bleeding, and vomiting and killed tens of thousands of people. For centuries there was no cure. Nor could it be prevented, because no one knew how it was transmitted. A Cuban physician named Carlos Finlay figured that out.

Finlay, who graduated from Jefferson Medical College in Philadelphia, theorized in the 1860s that yellow fever was caused by the *Aedes aegypti* mosquito. The medical community in Cuba paid no attention until 1901, when Finlay convinced Dr. Walter Reed, a U.S. Army surgeon given the job of ending yellow fever on the island of Cuba, then occupied by U.S. forces, to check if the theory was valid.

Reed performed controversial experiments with people who allowed themselves to get bitten by *Aedes aegypti*. Nearly all came down with yellow fever. Finlay was proven to be right. A U.S.-led sanitation campaign then eliminated stagnant water where the mosquitoes were breeding, and the viral disease disappeared.

continue ruling Cuba and Cubans who wanted to rule themselves, Ybor City's Hispanic population was politically divided.

José Martí in Florida

Martí's first speech in Florida took place in 1891 at the Liceo, one of Tampa's major Cuban social and political clubs. He was continuing his New York campaign to unite the veterans of the Ten Years' War with the younger generation. Because more black Cubans lived in Florida than in New York, Martí also spoke of racial unity. "Should we fear the black man, the generous black man, the black brother?" he said. "I know he has risen nobly as a column, firmly on the side of liberty . . . let others fear him. I love him."

The crowd gave him an ovation. He moved on to Key West a few days later. Key West had dozens of political clubs and a strong pro-independence feeling. But because there were so many different groups, Martí was concerned about infighting.

A marching band playing "La Bayamesa" ("The Woman from Bayamo"), the anthem written during the Ten Years' War and named after the town that was burned down in the fighting, welcomed him to Key West. One of the old veterans, José Francisco Lamadriz, embraced him.

"An *abrazo* (embrace) for the past revolution," said Martí.

"An *abrazo* for the new revolution," responded the old warrior.

A large crowd waving Cuban flags lined the route to Martí's hotel, and the San Carlos Institute was packed with Cubans who wanted to hear Martí.

Cuban patriot José Martí gave a speech to support Cuba on the steps of the Martínez Ybor cigar factory.

Beginning in 1891, Tampa and Key West became as important as New York in the struggle Martí was leading to free Cuba from colonial rule. He continued to live in New York and published *Patria* (Fatherland) from there. However, he started his Cuban Revolutionary Party in Key West. Most of the pro-independence Cuban political clubs joined Martí's party. He had won the trust of the community. That helped him also gain the trust of Máximo Gómez and Antonio Maceo—the generals with whom he had quarreled a decade earlier. Cubans in the United States who were followers of José Martí were ready to bring a war of independence to their island.

The plan called for three ships with a total of several hundred armed men to land in Cuba, where Martí had arranged for an uprising simultaneous with the landing. But in 1894, federal authorities broke up the plot near Jacksonville, Florida, as the expeditionaries waited for Martí to arrive from New York. The next year, Martí issued an order from his Front Street office in Manhattan and traveled to meet Gómez in the Dominican Republic. Martí's order was taken to Tampa and stashed inside a box of cigars destined for Cuba. It contained secret instructions authorizing the beginning of a new rebellion. On February 24, Cubans stormed several Spanish army installations—this marked the start of Cuba's War of Independence. On April 11, in a tropical downpour, Gómez, Martí, and four aides landed on the rocky coast of Playitas, on Cuba's far southeast. After all the years of plotting in the United States, Martí at last had brought the struggle to Cuba itself.

On May 19, however, Spanish soldiers shot and killed José Martí at a town called Dos Rios. He died without seeing his dream of an independent Cuba become real.

THE WAR OF INDEPENDENCE

Back in the United States, José Martí's successor as head of the Cuban Revolutionary Party was Tomás Estrada Palma, the director of a school in New York State's Central Valley attended by the children of well-to-do Hispanic families. Estrada Palma was a U.S. citizen, unlike Martí. He had been an officer in the Ten Years' War and was captured by the Spanish, but he escaped to New York and became a leader of the Cuban community in the United States. After Martí's death he was named representative in Washington, D.C., of the Cuban rebels. He became Cuba's first president in 1902.

Palma believed support from the United States was crucial for the Cuban cause and set out to win American sympathy, and organize Cuban fairs featuring proindependence speeches and photo exhibits of the war. He won the support of New York's *yellow press*. William Randolph Hearst's *Journal* and Joseph Pulitzer's *World* gave the war sensationalist coverage.

Cuba's first president, Tomás Estrada Palma.

The Cuban community in the United States continued to support the rebels. Fifteen armed expeditions left the United States for Cuba in 1896. That same year, Antonio Maceo, the veteran of the Ten Years' War Martí convinced to join the fighting again, carried the war to western Cuba, hundreds of miles beyond the place Gómez had fought for independence twenty years earlier. But he was killed in action. It was a blow to Cubans, but the war continued.

Spain put General Valeriano Weyler, whom Cubans still remember for his cruelty, in charge of crushing the rebellion. To deny the rebels help from peasants, he ordered that everyone living in the countryside move to camps set up in towns. Anyone who disobeyed would be executed. The camps were overwhelmed with poor families forced to leave their homes. Crops were not harvested, which resulted in devastating food shortages. New York newspapers carried pictures of starving children and stories of atrocities committed by Spanish troops, leading to calls for American military intervention.

Some Americans were genuinely appalled by conditions in Cuba, while others viewed Cuba in the same way that the Southwest had been viewed fifty years before—as a region that Manifest Destiny had reserved for the United States. Still others believed the United States should stay out of the conflict. Cubans were split, too. Some worried that if the United States entered the war, the Americans would not let Cuba become truly independent; others believed American troops would defeat Spain quickly and pave the way for Cuban independence.

Estrada Palma was caught in the middle. In 1898, he wrote, "The Cuban people do not now desire annexation. They are desirous that the American government in some manner manage to provide a guarantee for the internal peace of our country."

The different factions were still debating in February 1898, when the U.S. battleship *Maine*, sent to protect American interests, blew up in Havana harbor. New York newspapers blamed Spain and demanded the United States declare war. In late April, a joint congressional resolution authorized President William McKinley to force Spain out of Cuba, Puerto Rico, and the Philippines, the last remnants of a once vast empire. The war ended in just a few weeks with a decisive American victory. The United States ruled Cuba directly until 1902, when it became an independent country. But future dictatorships and corrupt governments would continue to send Cubans to the United States, seeking the freedom they did not have in their homeland.

The front page of the *New York Journal* for February 17, 1898.

People from many Latin American nations, not just Cuba, still come to the United States seeking freedom and opportunity—the U.S. Census estimated in 2006 there were 44.3 million Hispanics in the United States. What is not well known is that in the second half of the nineteenth century, along with the millions of immigrants from Germany, Ireland, Italy, and Eastern Europe, Hispanic Americans lived here, too, and helped to shape this country as well as their nations of origin.

TIMELINE

1492	Columbus discovers America.
1823	Father Felix Varela arrives in New York, works for Cuba's independence from Spain; he also ministers to poor European immigrants and becomes known as the Vicar of the Irish.
1830s	First Cuban cigar factory workers arrive in Key West.
1836	Texas breaks away from Mexico, declares itself an independent republic.
1845	United States annexes Texas as the twenty-eighth state, a cause for the war with Mexico.
1846	California declares itself an independent republic in June; one month later, the United States claims possession.
1848	United States-Mexico War ends; California and the South-western states ceded to the United States.
1849	General Mariano Vallejo helps write California state constitution; in New York, Cuban activist Narciso López designs the Cuban flag.
1850	New Mexico becomes a U.S. territory; California becomes a state; Narciso López, allied with pro-slavery Southerners, leads an unsuccessful armed attempt to free Cuba from Spanish rule and is executed by Spanish authorities after he is captured a year later.
1861	U.S. Civil War breaks out; some nine thousand soldiers of Hispanic origin fight in the conflict; Confederate troops from Texas take New Mexico.
1862	A largely Hispanic force wins New Mexico back for the Union.
1864	Admiral David G. Farragut, son of Spanish immigrants, gives his famous order, "Damn the torpedoes, full steam ahead!" during the battle of Mobile Bay.
1868	The start of Cuba's Ten Years' War for Independence sends thousands of emigrants to New York and Key West.
1874	New Mexico's territorial legislature passes a resolution asking for statehood; Congress votes down the proposal two years later.

1875	Romualdo Pacheco becomes the first, and thus far the only, Hispanic governor of California.
1879	Cuban national hero José Martí arrives in New York fleeing Spanish colonial authorities; he spends much of the next fifteen years in New York, Tampa, and Key West organizing Cuba's War of Independence.
1886	Cigar factory owner Vicente Martínez Ybor founds Ybor City, the beginnings of present-day Tampa.
1895	Cuba's War of Independence breaks out; José Martí is shot to death in a skirmish.
1896	A Supreme Court decision transfers to the federal government more than 6 million acres (2,428,113 ha) of land owned by Hispano villages in New Mexico.
1898	United States declares war on Spain; Cuba's War of Independence becomes known as the Spanish-American War, with eventual U.S. victory and independence for Cuba.
1912	New Mexico becomes a state.

GLOSSARY

absolutist king A monarch who rules without the constraint of laws.

anglos English-speaking Caucasian Americans not of Hispanic origin.

biculturalism Relating to two different cultures.

cede To give up something, especially territory.

congressional hearing A public meeting of Congress members to discuss proposed laws.

emancipate To free from slavery.

hispanics People who trace their ancestry to Spanish-speaking countries.

hispano New Mexicans who trace their ancestry to Spanish colonists (in Spanish, the word means Hispanic).

Manifest Destiny A mid-nineteenth-century political doctrine that said the United States should expand westward to the Pacific Ocean.

mestizos Persons of mixed Caucasian and Native-American descent.

militia A group of citizens trained for military service.

monarchial Related to kings and queens.

mulattoes Persons of mixed Caucasian and black ancestry.

Nuevomexicanos Early Spanish settlers of New Mexico.

posse A group of people organized temporarily to search for a fugitive.

reconstruction The period after the Civil War when the former Confederate states were reorganized for readmission to the Union.

sovereign An independent country.

speculators People who tried to buy land at low prices and sell it for a profit.

yellow press The sensationalist newspapers of the late nineteenth and early twentieth century.

xenophobia Fear or dislike of foreigners or anything that is foreign.

FURTHER INFORMATION

WEB SITES

Indiana University
www.latinamericanstudies.org/cubans-civil-war.htm
　　Cuban Americans in the Civil War

Institute of Texan Cultures Museum
www.texancultures.com
　　From the University of Texas at San Antonio

The National Hispanic Cultural Center
www.nhccnm.org
　　Part of the State of New Mexico's Department of Cultural Affairs

National Park Service
www.cr.nps.gov/history/online_books/5views/5views5.htm
　　History of Californios and Mexican immigrants in California

New Mexico Culturenet
www.nmculturenet.org
　　Artists, educators, writers, and technologists examine New Mexico's
　　history and culture

St. Petersburg Times
www.ybortimes.com/what-is-ybor.cfm
　　A guide to the history and present -day information for Ybor City

University of Texas at Austin
www.tsha.utexas.edu
　　The Handbook of Texas Online

Bibliography

De León, Arnoldo. *The Tejano Community, 1836-1900*. Albuquerque, NM: University of New Mexico Press, 1982. A history of Hispanics in Texas during the nineteenth century.

Hernández, Roger E., and Anton, Alex. *Cubans in America*. New York, NY: Kensington Books, 2002. An illustrated history of Cubans in the United States.

Montgomery, Charles. *The Spanish Redemption*. Berkeley and Los Angeles, CA: University of California Press, 2002. A history of New Mexico's Hispanos.

Mormino, Gary R., and Pozzetta, George E. *The Immigrant World of Ybor City*. Urbana and Chicago, IL: University of Illinois Press, 1987. A history of Cubans, Italians, and Spaniards in Tampa.

Nieto-Phillips, John M. *The Language of Blood*. Albuquerque, NM: University of New Mexico Press, 2004. Examines the cultural identity of Hispanos.

Orozco, Cynthia; Rocha, Rodolfo; and Zamora, Emilio, editors. *Americans in Texas History*. Austin, TX: Texas State Historical Association, 2000. A collection of essays on Mexican Americans in Texas.

Pitt, Leonard. *The Decline of the Californios*. Berkeley and Los Angeles, CA: University of California Press, 1966. A history of Spanish-speaking Californios, 1846-1890.

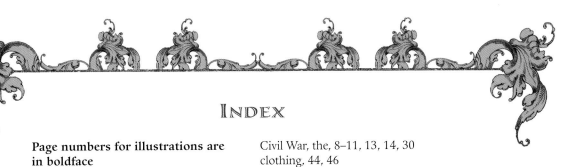

INDEX

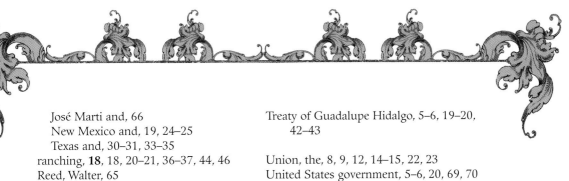

About the Author

ROGER E. HERNÁNDEZ writes a nationally syndicated column distributed by King Features to some forty daily newspapers across the country. He is also Writer in Residence at the New Jersey Institute of Technology and author of *Cubans in America*. Hernández was born in Cuba and came to the United States as a child in 1965, when his parents fled the Castro regime.